Whispers Of The Heart

Voices in Verse

Taronish Patel

Made with ❤ on the BookLeaf Publishing Platform
www.bookleafpub.in
www.bookleafpub.com

Dedication

To resonating with the emotions and reminiscing the experiences that transform fleeting moments into timeless verses.

Acknowledgement

This collection owes its existence to the infinite grace of the Divine. For the quiet moments of clarity and inspiration that brought these verses to life, I am profoundly grateful. I am beyond thankful for the love and encouragement of some incredible people. While I honour their request for anonymity, it would be remiss not to acknowledge who they are and what they mean to me.

To my parents, my unwavering pillars of belief and unconditional love— thank you for the literary gene and for making me pursue my penchant for poetry from the very beginning. To my sister, who has always been and will continue to be my ultimate source of undiluted joy and humour.
To the Love of my life, who redefines emotional endurance, loves gently, and Cheers for me Dedicatedly - Thank you!

Finally, to you, the reader — Thank you for opening this book and stepping into this shared space. Thank you for holding these poems in your hands and for allowing my words to find a home in your heart. I hope these words find you where you are and carry you to where you wish to be.

This book is as much yours as it is mine.

Preface

Firsts are always special, and this one is no exception. Poetry has long been my way of making sense of the world—its beauty, its chaos, and its quiet, transient moments. This book is a reflection of those experiences, shaped by love, faith, gratitude, delirious joy, grief, conflict, resilience, hope, renewal and growth. I wrote my first poem at 13 - a heartfelt expression of gratitude to my parents. Over the years, I have cherished crafting life-sized, handwritten, personalised poems as keepsakes ensconced in glass frames for a special few. After years of immersing myself in penning newsletter editorials, I look forward to fanning the flame of my poetic potential once again after about 15 years.

While I enjoy experimenting with free verse, I am especially drawn to the discipline of traditional forms / different types of poetry and rhyming verses, in particular, where constraints push me to be more inventive. For me, poetry is as much about the subtle yet sublime messaging as the words themselves; it's about what remains unsaid, waiting to be felt. While this compilation hinges on making relatability its central focus, it also hopes to induce those who would ordinarily lack the inclination to read big books, to give this one a go.

These pages don't aim to prescribe or validate the words they contain but are an invitation to have a dialogue with oneself. You may find your own stories within these lines or they may whisper something entirely unexpected to you. That is the magic of poetry—it lives anew with every reader; it echoes the fragments of our journeys so far, capturing a thought, a feeling, or a memory that demands attention and deserves to be shared.

Some of these poems were written in the solitude of long nights, others in the warmth of sunlight. Some emerged from moments of joy, while others were penned in hope for better days. Together, they weave a tapestry of moments that remind me, and perhaps you, that we are not alone, and that life, in all its wholeness and glory, is meant to be lived wholly.

The Poetry Project

I gather moments like stones, each one a
different weight,
Some skip across the surface, others sink deep
and ache to date.
In the quiet, I hear the echoes of what has
been and what could be,
Embers of memory burning soft beneath each
line of mighty praise and obloquy.

Between each line, there lies a silence,
different words that mean the same -
A breath, a pause, a fleeting flame.
We are maps drawn by stars, guided by scars,
Following a path through illuminated stars.

Unbeknownst to us, there are threads we
cannot see,
stitched by the passion for poetry.
they weave between the shadows of who we
were
And who we are destined to be.
This is my window- cracked and clear, wide
and bright -

A glimpse into love, loss, and the quiet pulse of night.

They dance in glances, in the spaces between,
A language unvoiced yet silently seen.
These are the verses of a heart untamed,
Wild and honest words, unashamed.

The Weave of Luck and Destiny

Luck and Destiny, threads entwined,
In patterns veiled from the human mind.
One, a whim- a wild, free chance,
The other, bound in ordered dance.

A coin that spins, a die that falls,
Luck laughs aloud in hallowed halls.
She shifts like wind, with fickle might,
A glance of fortune, a sudden light.

Destiny, with solemn gaze,
Walks through years, beneath our haze.
She waits in shadows, deep and still,
A quiet force, a patient will.

But are they foes or friends in guise?
One blinds the heart; one clears the eyes.
For every step that seems astray,
Is it Luck that leads, or Destiny's way?

When triumph comes, we call it fate,

As if the path was set, innate.
Yet stumble once, and Luck we blame,
A fickle ghost, ashamed by name.

They meet in moments small and vast,
A single thread, the first and last.
A wish fulfilled, a path unknown –
A life that's lived, a fate of its own.

So, hold them close, both whim and law,
The grasp of luck, the weight of awe.
For in their dance, we live and breathe,
A mystery only time can weave.

The Miracle of Love

True love blooms in quiet ways,
In sunlit hours and shadowed days.
It's in a glance that needs no sound,
A warmth that roots us to the ground.

It's gentle hands that ease our pain,
And laughter shared through joy and rain.
A kindness like the morning air,
That wraps around, unasked, yet there.

It's not a blaze that burns too bright,
But steady as the stars at night.
A glow that guides us, soft and clear,
In every heartbeat, always near.

In true love's eyes, we see our best,
A tender place, a welcome rest.
It lifts, it heals, it holds us true—
A gift, a grace, in all we do.

In every glance, in every trace,
A gentle touch, a soft embrace.
True love does not demand or take,

It nurtures all for kindness' sake.

A laugh that echoes, pure and clear,
A warmth that chases out all fear.
It lifts you up when shadows fall,
And answers swiftly, each fervent call.

It grows in silence, strong and bright,
A steady glow, a guiding light.
In every act, both small and grand,
True love is here to understand.

It does not fit logic; it defies the rules,
Confounding the wise, bemusing fools.
It needn't be measured by common sense,
For it is the weight of a special presence, the absence immense.

It needs no words, yet speaks aloud,
A heart that's humble, yet so proud.
For love that's true, both kind and wise,
In quiet grace it lives and helps us rise.

The Feather of Hope

Hope is a whisper in the dark,
A quiet spark, a momentary mark.
It stirs the soul when night is deep,
A promise made while others sleep.

It's fragile, yet it does not break,
A steady force for courage's sake.
Though winds may rage and storms descend,
Hope stands firm till the very end.

It's in the dawn that softly shows,
In every seed that slowly grows.
A strength unseen, yet always there,
A breath of faith in thinning air.

Hope doesn't waver, fade, or fall.
It's patient, constant through it all.
Through every trial, it will cope,
For life is born of endless hope.

It's the dawn that ends the night,
A ray of positivity, always in sight.
When despair looms, hope leads the way,

Turning every night into day.

Hope is a feather, light and true,
Carried on winds in skies so blue.
In times of storm, it gently sways,
A steady strength that mends our ways.

A Tumultuous Tango

In chambers deep, where thoughts reside,
The mind, with logic as its guide,
Charts each course with careful grace,
Its reason sharp, with measured pace.

But down below, the heart beats loud,
Unbound by reason, fierce and proud,
It surges wild, with passion bright,
A blaze of red, a star's delight.

The mind says, "Pause; let sense prevail.
For whims can lead your steps to fail."
It speaks in tones both calm and clear,
Its voice, a shield against our fear.

Yet heart replies, "To live, one must feel,
To dive beneath the cold, hard steel."
It pulses strong, demands to dare,
To chase its dreams in adversity's glare.

The heart and mind did clash one day,
In a storm where reason lost its sway.
The mind, with logic sharp and keen,

Declared, "I rule! My reign supreme!"

They wrestle thus, a constant fight,
Through dawn's new glow and silent night—
A dance of two, a tug of war,
The mind to keep, the heart to soar.

But deep within, the heart replied,
"A truth exists you can't override.
For while your laws may chart the skies,
I live in dreams, where passion flies."

The mind, though proud, began to wane,
For love defied its cold domain.
In every beat, the heart would show,
It had a mind the mind can't know.

So, logic bowed, and let it be,
The heart, now free, claimed victory.
For wisdom lives where feelings bloom,
And the heart and mind find shared room.

Beyond the Bitter Hold

A grudge is weight upon the soul,
A stone that never lets you be whole.
It buries joy, it steals the light,
And turns your world from day to night.

It festers deep within the chest,
A wound that never finds its rest.
It clouds the heart with bitter rain,
And wraps the mind in endless pain.

Yet in its grasp, we hold so tight,
Believing it will set things right.
But time, like water, wears it thin—
A lesson learned too late to win.

For grudges only bind the free,
A cage in which one cannot see.
To let them go is to release,
The soul's own path to quiet peace.

So drop the stone, let shadows fade,
And let your heart be unafraid.
For in forgiveness, we are whole,

And only love can heal the soul.

What weight is borne by bitter hearts,
When grudges fester, leaving marks?
A flame we hold, but not to light,
It burns within, unseen, in spite.

Old wounds unhealed are chains we wear,
Invisible, yet everywhere.
We drag them forth from day to day,
But find no comfort along the way.

For grudges grow, a shadow cast,
Binding us close to pain long past.
Each slight we guard, each hurt we keep,
Is stolen from the joy we seek.

What gain, what good, in bitter aims,
In tethered souls and silent blames?
When grudges fade, a burden lifts,
And life reclaims its stifled gifts.

Release the fire, let embers die,
Forgiveness frees and wings the sky.
For life is brief, too uncertain and strange,

To bear the weight of wounds in exchange.

Wounds of Misinterpretation: Keep them within

A glance too quick, a word misplaced and of waste,
A silence born of thoughtless haste.
Like thunder from a cloudless sky,
A simple spark can multiply.

Each meaning twisted, warped by fear,
What once was close feels distant here.
Unspoken doubts begin to grow,
In shadows, the heart could not even know.

Yet in this rift, multiple lessons hide,
A chance to look past wounded pride.
To find the truth beneath the ache—
The strength that only understanding can make.

A look unseen, a phrase unknown,
And suddenly, we're both alone.

Those once close now stand apart,
Divided by wounds of a misread heart.

For in the end, what heals this pain
Is listening close to each refrain.
The power lies not in the sting,
But in the mending love can bring.

The world is not our stage to cry,
To seek respite or question why.
In showing wounds for all to see,
We only feed a crowd that never sets us free.

True wisdom lies in quiet grace,
Not every scar needs public space.
To bare those demons, raw and wild,
Is to regress, not reconcile.

Insecurities, we all possess,
But broadcasting them adds to distress.
Public validation is not what should be craved,
For a path of strength and grace is what ought to be paved.

True resolve blooms deep inside,
Where courage and calmness coincide.
The mature soul learns to stand,
Not with foolish cries, but a steady hand.

The Shifting Gaze

When your stars align, and success takes flight,
You're bathed in warmth, in the dazzling spotlight.
Faces turn, hands reach your way,
Praises rise like the break of day.

Your steps are strong, your voice is clear,
The world's embrace tightens with every cheer.
Smiles widen, heads nod in sync,
A moment awaits, and you are on the brink.

But fail, stumble, or lose your grace,
And watch the warmth turn cold and space.
Eyes once bright now cast askance,
As if your worth were mere circumstance.

Words fall silent, whispers grow,
They watch, they judge, from shadows low.
Each step feels heavy, each breath feels weighed,
In the absence of light, loyalties fade.

Success brings friends like moths to flame,
But failure's shadow sifts the same.
In the ebb and flow, some shy while others stand tall,
True faces shine, while masks may fall.

For in the silence of defeat's embrace,
You learn who stands and who leaves the race.
And when you rise from what you've seen,
You'll know who is true and who's routine.

When success arrives, the world takes note,
Your name is praised, your words they quote.
The doors swing wide, the paths are clear,
And everyone gathers, from far and near.

But when you're down, without a dime,
The silence echoes a harsh paradigm.
The crowd once loud now fades away,
And eyes that once sparkled now quickly stray.

In triumph, you're the shining star,
In struggle, just a step too far.

The shift is subtle, yet clear as glass,
A difference felt as moments pass.

For in the end, it's not the praise,
But the strength you find through darker days.
Success may come, and fame may fade,
But your true value is never swayed.

Yet, through it all, one truth remains—
The gaze that matters is not theirs to gain.
It's the look you give yourself, with grace,
When you find your worth, no matter the place.

The Triumphant Truth

In the heart, where truth resides,
Beyond the tide of fleeting strides,
There lies a force both pure and strong,
That guides the soul when winds are wrong.

It does not seek the world's applause,
Nor chase the cursory, hollow cause.
For all who walk the honest way,
Will greet the dawn of a brighter day.

True intentions, steady and clear,
May wander roads both far and near,
But in their wake, they leave a trace
Of kindness, love, and lasting grace.

They are the roots that grow unseen,
In fields of hope, through spaces green.
Though storms may test, and time may bend,
True intentions triumph in the end.

Those who constantly preach the cosmic law,
May not be entirely free of flaw.
The commentary, endless and too vain,

Adds no weight to the law's supreme reign.

The truly just, they seek no fight,
They walk with kindness as their light.
They do not claim the judge's throne,
For they know that justice rides alone.

For they are pure, they never sway,
And in their light, we find our way.
So let the world around us spin and have its
whims—
True triumph lies where truth begins.

The Alchemy of Dreams

The soul sets softly in the shroud of night,
A sudden shadow lost to fading light.
Its whispers drown in silence deep,
A thousand stars unable to weep.

Yet in the dark, where echoes lay,
The seeds of dawn begin to play.
A spark ignites, a secret fire,
Fanned by dreams and quiet desire.

Though weighed by sorrow's somber hue,
The soul remembers skies of blue.
In shadow's grip, it learns to fight,
To rise again, reborn in light.

Each fall a chapter, each wound in time,
Each tear, a prism, a truth divine.
For darkness molds the strength it needs,
To bloom again from buried seeds.

Beneath the moon's soft, silver glow,
A secret magic starts to grow.
Through whispered winds and ancient trees,

Emerges the alchemy of mysteries.

Transforming shadows into light,
It dances softly through the night.
A spark becomes a blazing flame,
And nothing ever stays the same.

The heart, a cauldron deep and wide,
Holds hopes and fears we cannot hide.
But through this alchemy, we see,
The path to who we're meant to be.

So let the stars weave spells above,
And fill the night with fearless love.
For in this life's vast symphony,
Our souls are bound by alchemy.

And when the morning splits the sky,
The soul ascends, no longer shy.
From ashes forged, it soars in flight,
Once lost in darkness, now alive in light.

Flawed Judgement

They point their fingers, cast their blame,
Quick to decide, quick to name.
A glance, a whisper, a fading clue—
And suddenly, they thought they knew.

The book unread, a place unexplored, the tale untold,
Dismissed before any facts unfold.
A single page, a single line,
And yet they claim the whole design.

But time, relentless, lifts the veil,
Revealing more to every tale.
What seemed so clear, so black, so white,
Was shaded gray in broader light.

The kind they scorned, the weak they mocked,
Held strength and grace that left them shocked.
The ones they praised, so high, so proud,
Were proven hollow when truth allowed.

Oh, how the hasty build their walls,
Blind to the lessons when judgment calls.
For wisdom waits, it does not run—
Its work begins when ours is done.

Caught in the storm, not the maker of rain,
Held captive by fate, bound tight by its chain.
Yet whispers of blame rise sharp and unkind,
Judged for the scars, not the story behind.

Misunderstood, they carry the weight of the world, blind to their pain,
Judging the surface, not the scars they sustain.
But as the truth unwinds, the world's guilt revealed,
They see the context, and sorrow is forever healed.

Judge less the path you've never walked,
Where presumptive whispers cruelly talked.
For kindness, soft, will always prove,
It's the strongest force which makes the heart move.

Let empathy replace the urge to blame,

No soul is perfect, none the same.
For when you choose to judge no more,
Your world will finally begin to soar.

So, meet with wonder, leave room for grace,
Let time reveal the fuller face.
A world of nuance waits to show,
That first impressions rarely know.

All in Good Time

The clock may tick, the days may flee,
Yet all unfolds as it should be.
Though storms may rise, and skies may cry,
The sun returns, the clouds drift by.

We plant the seeds, we dream, we yearn,
But growth demands it's time to turn.
A flower blooms not at our will—
It opens when the world is still.

The stars align, though we can't see,
A higher plan for you and me.
The winding path, the unseen way,
Will lead us where we're meant to stay.

Impatience demands, "Hurry! Strive!"
Yet peace is where true faith can thrive.
For what is ours will find its way,
In perfect time, on a perfect day.

Each tear, a thread in destiny's loom,
Weaving a union that now finds bloom.
The clock's stern hands try to divide,

But in good timing's embrace is where trust should reside.

So here they stand, unbroken, true,
A journey complete yet starting anew.
Time, tests, tribulations, all left behind,
A union blessed by hearts aligned.

So, trust the flow, release the fight,
Let shadows dance their way to light.
For life unfolds with grace divine,
Each moment stitched in sacred time.

Inspiration is Omnipresent

In every breath, in every glance,
In whispers soft, or a storm's dance,
In golden dawn or midnight's hue,
Inspiration waits, in shadows too.

It hides in laughter, bold and bright,
In silence wrapped in calm twilight,
In creeks that sing, in clouds that drift,
A boundless, ceaseless, unseen gift.

It's in the lines on weathered hands,
In shifting tides, in windswept sands,
In autumn's burn, in spring's rebirth,
In all that lives upon this earth.

A spark that leaps, a voice that calls,
In every rise, in every fall,

Wherever minds and hearts may roam,
Inspiration makes its quiet home.

In leaves that tremble on the breeze,
In roots entwined beneath the trees,
In drops of rain, in grains of sand,
Inspiration waits, close at hand.

It's in the pulse of city streets,
In strangers' eyes, in friends we meet,
In candle glow and a starlit sky,
In hidden paths where wonders lie.

In laughter shared, in sorrow's grace,
In every line of every face,
In echoes of a whispered dream,
It's woven deep in every seam.

In quiet dawns, in fierce goodbyes,
In rivers running soft and wise,

It threads through all that breathes and sings—

For inspiration lives in everything.

Life as a Balance Sheet

Life is like a balance sheet,
With assets, debts, and moments sweet.
Each day we tally, each choice we make,
A ledger where both joy and heartache stake.

On one side, dreams and love accrue,
A wealth of moments, bright and true.
Today's time is in their favour,
But tomorrow's will be ours to savor.

On the other, losses and the cost,
The times we stumble, things we've lost.
Yet even in the darkest hours,
These too are part of life's true powers.

The credit is the kindness given,
The debits come from roads we've ridden,
But balance comes when we can see

That both the highs and lows shape life's tree.

So at the end, when all is tallied and aligned,
The sheet is balanced, no one's left maligned.
For life is about the rise and the fall —
It's what we learn and give to all.

Embracing Imperfections

In the cracks and the flaws, the beauty resides,
Not in perfection, but where the light hides.
Each jagged edge tells a story untold,
Of moments too raw, of hearts made of gold.

The crooked smile, the scar on the skin,
Are not marks of weakness but strength within.
For in imperfection, we find our own grace,
A rhythm that's ours, no need to chase.

The unfinished lines, the quiet mistake,
Are parts of the whole that we dare not forsake.
For we are not meant to be flawless, complete—
We are meant to be human, tender, and sweet.

So let go of the chase, the desire to hide,

And embrace what is real, what cannot be denied.

For in our imperfections, we truly become,

The truest version of all we've ever been.

In the spaces where flaws take their place,

We find beauty and gentle grace.

Not in the perfect, the polished and bright,

But in the cracks where shadows find light.

The rough edges, the scars we bear,

Are marks of a life we've lived, laid bare.

Each misstep, each tear that falls,

Becomes part of the story that calls.

We are not made of flawless design,

But of moments imperfect, by choice divine.

For in the broken, there's room to grow,

A truth that we learn as we learn to show.

So, embrace the crooked, the untamed, the real,
For in our flaws, our hearts begin to heal.
We are beautiful not despite, but because,
Of the imperfections that shape who we are.

Wholeness blooms in what we bear,
In tender mercies and moments rare.
It is not perfection, but the soul –
Embracing it all to make us whole.

The Complete Woman

She walks with grace, yet knows her might,
A blend of softness, strength, and light,
Her heart a compass, pure and true,
Guiding herself and others too.

She speaks with power, gentle, clear,
Her words are a melody to hear,
Yet listens deep, with open ear,
Understanding all and holding near.

Her mind is sharp, a world of thought,
In wisdom's depths, she's always sought.
But she's not just the words she says,
She lives the truth in all her ways.

She loves with depth, with hands that heal,
A warmth that's endless, kind, and real,
Her love, a fire that softly grows,

It nurtures all and always knows.

She wears her scars like precious art,
Each one a mark upon her heart.
For every wound has made her whole,
A testament to her strong soul.

A complete woman is not one thing,
She's all the songs the wild birds sing.
The strength to rise, the grace to fall,
In every way, she gives her all.

To be a woman, whole and true,
Is not just what the world might view,
It's strength within, both soft and strong,
A balance found where hearts belong.

It takes the courage to stand tall,
To rise above, to sacrifice it all,
With grace, with fire, with gentle might,
A woman shines in the darkest of nights.

It takes the wisdom to know when,
To speak with power, to listen then,
To build, to dream, to break the mould,
With stories of the brave and bold.

It takes the kindness to forgive,
To understand, to truly live,
To love with depth, to lift with care,
To be a light when none is there.

It takes the heart to feel the ache,
And still move forward, for love's sake.
To own the scars, the joy, the pain,
And find the strength to rise again.

A complete woman is not defined
By others' views, but by her mind,
Her heart, her spirit, fierce and free,
She is, and always will be, she.

The Shadow of Thought

Beneath the mind's quiet stream,
Dark ripples stir, a subtle gleam.
A fleeting doubt, a whispered shade,
The seeds of harm unwittingly laid.

To think ill of another's soul
Chips away at our own whole.
The heart grows heavy, weighed with spite,
Its glow diminished, dimmed of light.

What harm can thoughts alone impart?
They forge the pathways of the heart.
A fleeting scorn, a silent curse,
Can turn kind moments into worse.

The bonds we share, so fine, so frail,
Are marred by thoughts that weave a veil.
Of mistrust, anger, baseless fear,

Turning friend to stranger, once near.

But should we pause, should grace take hold,
And let compassion, pure and bold,
Sweep through the chambers of our mind,
We'll leave the shadows far behind.

For every soul is flawed, like clay,
Yet moulded still in love's own way.
Think not of faults, but gifts they bring,
And hear the tune their spirits sing.

Release the chains of thoughts unkind,
And find the peace that's hard to find.
For in each heart, a mirror lies,
Reflecting what we choose to prize.

Respect's Two-Way Street

Respect is not a gift bestowed,
Nor something earned by forceful code.
It's built on trust, on mutual care,
A bond that grows when both hearts share.

A two-way street, its path is clear,
Where kindness walks with those who steer.
It cannot thrive on one alone,
But flourishes when seeds are sown.

To give respect, one must receive,
For balance helps both souls to believe.
A word, a deed, a gentle tone,
Can light the bridge where love is shown.

Yet should one side the effort shirk,
The fragile threads no longer work.

For walls arise when pride takes hold,
And hearts retreat, grown distant, cold.

Tread this road with humble stride,
Let patience, grace, and truth abide.
For in the mirror of your way,
Respect reflects both night and day.

The Lens of Perspectives

The world we see is never clear,
A mirror bent by love and fear.
What feels so right may still belong,
To those who deem it wholly wrong.

A thousand eyes, a thousand skies,
Each holds its truths, its sacred ties.
The stories clash, yet move along,
For no one's right, and no one's wrong.

The steps we take, the roads we tread,
Are painted hues inside our head.
And though our views may not belong,
The heart beats neither right nor wrong.

So, pause and hear another's way,
Their night, their dawn, their shades of gray.
Through different eyes, the world is known,

Each view unique, each seed its own.

A river flows where paths divide,
Each traveller walks with a steadfast stride.
Their truths, though varied, still belong,
For none can claim they're wholly wrong.

The stars above may shift and sway,
Yet light the skies in their own way.
Each heart beats fierce, its rhythm strong,
A melody of right and wrong.

Temporary Tears

Tears fall like rain, soft and fleeting,
A release that carries weight for a moment.
They do not last long,
But in their brief presence, there is a quiet cleansing.

Each drop is a fragment of emotion,
A passing storm within the soul.
They gather without warning,
And then, just as quickly, they begin to fade.

There is no shame in their arrival,
No need to understand their cause.
They simply flow,
A natural release, a temporary surrender.

In the space between their fall and absence,
There is a gentle softness,
A reminder that pain is transient,
And that even sorrow has an end.

The face grows still once more,
The eyes dry, the heart settles,

But the weight lifted remains,
Even after the tears have vanished.

These tears are not forever,
They do not mark the end.
They are only moments,
A brief touch of vulnerability before moving on.

Like clouds that pass without a trace,
Tears too leave no lasting mark,
Only the quiet truth that we are human,
And that it is okay to feel, even if it's for a while.

Temporary as they are, they teach us,
That nothing stays, neither joy nor grief.
Tears remind us that we can endure,
That we can be whole, even in fleeting moments of brokenness.

Real is Rare

To be real is to stand upright in the quiet truth,
Not hidden behind masks or polished facades.
It is to speak with the rawness of the heart,
Unfiltered, unguarded, vulnerable in the open air.

It is in the cracks of imperfection,
In the moments of doubt, of uncertainty,
Where the strength of being real is found,
In the courage to show up, just as we are.

The world will offer masks of ease,
Telling us to fit in, to conform,
But realness does not seek approval,
It thrives in the spaces between the expectations.

Being real is not always neat,
It's messy, uncomfortable,
Yet it is the truest form of freedom,
To let go of the pretense and simply breathe.

In the quiet acceptance of our own flaws,
In the honest recognition of our growth,
We find the peace of being whole,
Not perfect, but real.

To be real is to exist without disguise,
To stand firm in the quiet knowing of oneself,
Not shaped by the opinions of others,
But by the truth that lives beneath the
surface.

It is to speak from the core,
Where the rawness of feeling flows freely,
Without concern for judgment or
expectation,
Just the simplicity of being fully present.

Realness does not ask for acceptance,
It does not seek validation,
It simply is, unashamed of its own
complexity,
In its fallibility, it finds its power.

There is no need for pretense,
No space for illusions,

Only the honest unfolding of who we are,
In every moment, unapologetically.

To be real is not easy,
It is a firm rebellion,
A return to what is genuine,
In a world that often asks for something else.

Healing in the Rain

Dancing in the rain is an act of surrender,
The cool droplets kiss the skin,
A gentle reminder that there is grace in release,
That healing comes not through control, but through flow.

Each step in the wet earth,
A movement towards letting go,
The rhythm of the storm syncs with the heart,
And for a moment, the world pauses with you.

The sky weeps, and so do you,
But the dance does not stop,
It is a release, a softening,
A way to become whole again through the rawness of the moment.

The rain does not judge,
It falls without hesitation,
And in its embrace, the wounds find space to breathe,

To be washed, to be cleansed, to be freed.

In the act of dancing, the body heals,
The soul finds a rhythm it had forgotten,
And the storm, though loud and fierce,
Becomes a quiet balm for the heart.

In the rain, there is an assuring invitation,
A call to move, to release what's heavy.
Waterfalls in sheets,
And each drop is a story of letting go.

With each step, the earth shifts beneath,
Mud clings to feet, but the body does not
resist.
The cold and warmth collide,
And in contrast, something begins to soften.

The sky opens its heart,
Not in anger, but in compassion,
Washing away the unspoken weight,
As if the storm itself knows the need for
renewal.

There is no rush, no perfect form,

Just the freedom of being,
The dance a language of its own,
Spoken through movement, through breath,
through rain.

Healing does not demand,
It simply unfolds, like the rhythm of water,
Finding its way into the cracks,
Making space for something new to emerge.

Generosity of the Universe

The universe gives without asking,
A soft breeze that carries life,
The light of stars scattered across the dark,
Endless, unmeasured, always there.

Mountains rise and fall in silence,
A rhythm older than time itself,
Oceans stretch far beyond sight,
Whispering secrets to the shore.

The earth cradles every seed,
Nurturing with patience, with care,
In every moment, it gives,
Without condition, without expectation.

The sky, vast and open,
Holds both storm and calm,
Each season unfolds its gifts,
A quiet generosity shared with all.

And we, small and fleeting,

Are part of this boundless flow,
Caught in the grace of giving,
The universe, always giving, always free.

Hotel Happiness

There is a place where doors stand wide,
Each room, a space where joy resides.
No check-in forms, no luggage to carry,
Just moments of peace that arrive like a
breeze.

The walls hum with laughter, soft and free,
And windows let in light that never fades.
The hallways are long, but never lonely,
Every step a song, every glance a smile.

Here, time drifts without burden,
Hours seem to fold into themselves.
In each corner, there's a quiet warmth,
Like the promise of tomorrow, just beyond
reach.

Guests come and go without need for keys,
There's no hurry, no rush to check out.
They stay as long as their hearts can hold,
And leave when their spirits are full.

No walls separate one from another,

Every soul, in harmony with the next.
Whispers of kindness float through the air,
The kind of language only the heart can
understand.

At the Hotel of Happiness, you are free—
Not to possess, but simply to be.
In this place, all needs dissolve,
And in the end, we find that bliss was always
here.

Fragile Love, True Love

Love, they say, is fragile,
a glassy wisp of light,
it glimmers in the morning,
but dims by the night.

A whispered word, an ephemeral glance,
a touch too soft to stay,
it teeters on the edge of loss,
so quick to fade away.

Yet, in the quiet, steadfast hearts,
true love begins to grow,
not born of fleeting passions,
but a steady, warming glow.

It weathers storms and bitter winds,
and roots in soil deep,
it holds the soul through shadowed nights,
when weaker hearts might weep.

True love is forged in trial's flame,
a tempered, steady steel,
unbreakable, enduring,

it's the love that's truly real.

True love, poured neat,
never diluted or masked, it cuts through all
the senses,
strong, unyielding,
leaving its mark long after the glass is empty.

It is a drink we dare not rush,
sipping slowly,
aware that its fragility,
makes each moment all the more precious.

Yet even the finest concoction,
when held too tightly,
may slip through our fingers,
disappearing before we know it.

So let the fragile fancies fade,
like petals in the breeze,
for love that's strong will rise above,
and last through centuries.

The Quintessential Outfit

It wears no seams, no tailored edge,
yet cloaks the soul in brilliance.
A fabric unseen, woven from threads
of longing, courage, and surrender.

Its color shifts with the turning sun—
dawn's quiet blush,
noon's blazing certainty,
twilight's dusky embrace.

Each hue a whisper, a declaration,
a secret told in light.
No jewels adorn this attire,
yet it gleams.

Not with gold or crystal,
but with the weightless shimmer
of truth,
of trust,
of touch.

It is both armor and vulnerability,
a shield that bares
the tenderest places.
Its folds carry the scent
of skin,
of earth,
of something eternal.

When it is worn,
it cannot be seen.
When it is shed,
it leaves no trace.
Yet it lingers,
an echo in the heart,
a warmth beneath the ribs.

This is the garment
we wear into the world,
or leave hanging
in the quiet corners of ourselves—
the outfit of love,
of splendour,
of what it means to be whole.

Not stitched by hands,

but by the breath of promises
and the weight of silences held too long.
It is made of moments—
a gaze,
a fingertip brushing the edge of hope,
the shiver of a name whispered in the dark.

It glows, not with borrowed light,
but with the quiet fire
of something unbroken.
Not flawless, but whole.

It fits all bodies
and none.
A fabric that clings to truth,
yet slips from those who grasp too tightly.

Invisible to the eye,
it is felt in the spaces between,
where love rests,
soft and heavy,
against the fragile architecture of the heart.

An outfit without shape,
without end.

It is worn,
not to be seen,
but to be known.

Overcoming Fear

Fear is a shadow that grows in silence,
a weight that presses, unseen,
clinging to the edges of the heart.
It whispers, urging retreat,
telling you to stay small,
to stay hidden.

But there is something in the body that stirs,
something that rises like dawn,
and with it comes the quiet strength
to step forward,
even when the path is unclear.

It begins with a breath,
a single act of courage,
that grows into a force
stronger than the doubt that once held you.
And slowly, fear shrinks
as you stretch toward the unknown,
as you stand tall in the face of what once felt
too large,
learning that it was never as powerful
as it pretended to be.

To overcome fear is to realize
that it does not own you—
you are the one who chooses
to walk through the dark
and find the light.

Fear is a shadow that stretches wide,
A silent whisper that clings to the mind,
A weight upon the chest that never quite lifts,
A puzzle with no edges, no corners to find.

But step by step, a hand reaches out,
Not for safety, but for the unknown,
With every breath, a new ground is touched,
A story of courage is quietly grown.

The heart that once trembled learns to beat
strong,
And the chains that once bound, begin to
fade,
For in the face of what frightens,
We are often unmade, and then remade.

Fear, in its power, starts to retreat,

Not conquered by force, but by simply being,
And in the stillness that follows the storm,
We discover a strength we never thought we possessed.

Who is Home?

Who is home, we might wonder and roam,
It's the place where we are loved, never left
alone.
With a smile and cheer,
It's the ones we hold dear,
Home is wherever we are truly known.

Self-worth, Self-love

To value oneself is to stand firm in silence,

Not needing the world's approval to know one's worth.

It is a quiet confidence that grows from within,

Rooted deep in the acceptance of who you are.

It is not the loudest voice that commands respect,

But the steady, grounded presence of knowing.

Value is not earned by comparison,

It is discovered by honouring the self in its entirety.

There is never a need to seek validation from others,

For the worth you carry does not change with opinions.

It is intrinsic, unshakable,

A truth that resides in the quiet space between thoughts.

To value oneself is to embrace imperfections,

To see flaws as part of the unique whole.

It is a compassion that flows inward,

A tenderness offered to the soul in its most raw form.

Value comes in the simple act of showing up,

Of choosing to be present, without doubt or hesitation.

It is in the courage to honour your boundaries,

And in the grace of forgiving yourself when you falter.

To value oneself is to recognize that you are enough,

Not in a world defined by external measures,

But in the understanding that your being is worthy,

Just as it is, in this moment, and every moment to come.

The Joy of Being a Child Again

To be a child again is to wake,
with the promise of newness in the air,
the heaviness of yesterday,
not yet weighing on your shoulders.

It is the innocence of curiosity,
without fear of the answers.
The curiosity that sees no limit,
no boundary, no "not yet."

It's in the small hands that hold the world,
with an understanding so pure,
believing a hug can heal,
and laughter can silence all worry.

It's running through the world,
as if it were made just for you,

as if there are no obstacles,

but only places to discover

and wonders to uncover.

To be a child again

is to forget the rules

and remember the magic of being alive.

To be a child again is to find joy in the smallest things—

the way the sunlight dances on the leaves,

the feel of rain as it taps softly on your skin,

the rush of wind promising freedom with each breath.

It is the unmeasured hours,

when time is not a thief but a companion,

and play is a language of its own,

spoken without care, without rule.

It is the laughter that bubbles up,

from a place that needs no reason,
the excitement of each new discovery,
as though the world is a treasure chest,
waiting to be opened.

To be a child again
is to trust in the beauty of simplicity,
to find contentment in small wonders,
and to carry joy within,
without questioning where it came from.

The Power of Prayer

A voice,
not always loud,
but steady as a pulse,
rises into the dark,
where no one watches,
yet everything listens.

It is not a command,
not a plea,
but a thread unwinding,
a whisper stitched in silence,
binding the heart to something vast,
something unseen.

When words fail,
it moves through breath,
through tears,
through the quaking of hands

clasped as though holding
the edge of the infinite.

Prayer does not alter the sun,
nor stop the tides,
nor unbend time's relentless arc.
But it reshapes the air within the soul,
so it carries a different weight.

And though the world
may remain untouched,
the one who prays
emerges—
lighter,
stronger,
unbroken.

The Pulse of Life

Each morning, the sun presses its warmth
against the earth's skin,
whispering a promise:
this day is yours.

Step forward, unafraid of falling.
Feel the weight of the wind,
the sharp sweetness of rain,
the ground firm beneath your reaching.

Do not measure life by the miles you walk
or the hours you endure.
It is in the way your laughter spills over,
how your silence holds meaning,
the tenderness you carve into the world.

Be boundless,
a river rushing without regret,

a fire that consumes without hesitation.

Let life unfold in your hands—
its beauty, its ache,
its brief and infinite wonder.

Breathe deeply,
feel the rhythm beneath your ribs,
a quiet drumbeat reminding you—
this moment is alive.

Walk barefoot on the edge of risk,
taste the salt of your own daring.
Let the horizon pull you forward,
its light shifting with every step.

Speak truths that tremble on your tongue.
Hold the weight of another's hand
as if it anchors you to the earth.

Know the sting of failure,

the rise of hope,
the fragile balance between them.

Life is not a map to be followed;
it is the pulse in your chest,
the leap into what comes next.

Fulfilled Promises: The Best Keepsakes

A promise is not a whisper to the wind,
but a stone placed in another's hand.
It has weight.
It remembers where it was set down,
aching in the absence of follow-through.

The world is littered with words
that never found their shape.
Empty phrases, like broken bridges,
spanning nothing.

To act is to carve truth
from the soft clay of intention.
To follow through is to honour the gravity
of what we dare to give voice to.

Let us not speak

what we cannot hold.
For promises are not merely made;
they are built—
and the unbuilt crumble
into silence.

A promise is not a fleeting breath,
but a seed pressed into the earth,
waiting for the rain of action.
Without care, it withers,
its roots never touch the truth.

Words are easy,
soft as feathers floating in the air.
But what are they
without the weight of hands
to bring them down to soil,
to make them real?

A promise broken
is not forgotten;

it lingers,
a hollow echo in the chambers
of those who trusted.

To act is to give life to our words,
to let them stand as trees,
strong against the shifting winds.
For a promise fulfilled
is not just an act of truth—
It is a gift of honour.

The Core of Inner Strength

Strength is not the shout in a crowded room,
but the silent resolve to stand firm
when the winds howl in dissent.

It is patience,
the ability to wait without bitterness,
while time carves its path through uncertainty.

Strength is humility,
the wisdom to kneel
so that others may rise,
knowing that lifting another
lifts us all.

It is kindness—
not soft, not weak,

but deliberate and enduring,
a shield against the world's indifference.

Strength is honesty,
even when truth cuts sharper
than the blunt ease of a lie.

It is resilience,
not in avoiding the fall,
but in rising, battered yet unbroken,
each scar a testament
to the power of persistence.

Strength is magnanimity,
to forgive someone
who was not apologetic,
to accept an apology
that was never received.

It is love,
unconditional and fierce,

a force that binds us
even when all else unravels.

The Right Balance

In life's intricate web, balance is grand,
Too much or too little can never stand.
With temperate care,
We thrive and repair,
An equilibrium to live a life as planned.

A Moment to Mend

A contrite heart, with words deftly spun,
Seeks to mend what was said, not undone.
In the art of regret,
A true *mea culpa* is set—
An embrocation for the wounds of a battle once won.

A Sonnet on Silence (a.k.a. Absence)

In silent chambers where no breath remains,
The echoes linger, though no voice is near.
A spectral song that travels through the veins,
Reminding hearts of what they held most dear.

Absence, a shadow cast by vanished light,
Consumes the space where once a presence burned.
It fills the soul with melancholy's blight,
A lesson taught, yet never fully learned.

Oh, quiet void, your whispers intertwine
With memory's touch, both tender and unkind.
The clock's soft ticking draws no steadfast line,

For time can't heal what absence leaves behind.

Yet in the stillness, truth begins to rise:

The heart endures, though silence fills its skies.

The Pillar of Trust

When shadows fall and doubts arise,
A beacon calls the way.
Trust is the lamp that lights the path,
Through nights that seem to sway.

It binds the hearts of souls entwined,
A silent, sacred bond.
In honesty, its roots are set,
To nurture and respond.

Without it, bridges turn to dust,
And walls are built in vain.
But trust, once nurtured, is the key
To break the chains of pain.

A whispered promise, soft and true,
Can heal a thousand scars.
It holds the power to restore

What time has marred with wars.

For trust is more than fleeting words,
It's action's steady hand.
A fortress built on faith and hope,
A force that will withstand.

The fragile heart, when trust is lost,
Is shattered, torn apart.
Yet when repaired, it beats anew,
Revived by love's true art.

To place one's faith within another
Is not a fleeting whim.
It's a legacy that echoes loud
In every choice we've pinned.

Through storm and strife, in every trial,
Trust stands the test of time.
It is the rhythm in the dance,
A quiet, steady rhyme.

Treasure trust, that precious gem,
Its value cannot wane.
For with it, we unlock the door
To joy that liberates us from pain.

The Ascent of Victory

Upon the peak, where victors proudly stand,
A beam shines, igniting envious gaze.
For success begets a path both broad and grand,
Its golden lure a fire to amaze.

Each triumph builds a stair to greater heights,
A testament to perseverance shown.
Momentum gathers with each earned delight,
As glory claims a kingdom of its own.

Adversity, though fierce, must yield in time,
To those who wield their will as tempered steel.
Success becomes the rhythm and the rhyme,
A force the doubters cannot help but feel.

Through effort honed, the fortunate ascend,
Each laurel earned a herald to the next.

The cycle turns, as victors comprehend,
That triumph writes the language of the text.

No guide can teach the steps success must trace,
For each ascent is carved by one alone.
Yet once the summit meets the climber's face,
The world bestows its favour on the throne.

Success, a siren, calls to kindred hearts,
Its echoes drawing others to its flame.
A catalyst, where enterprise imparts,
The power to transform a fleeting name.

Thus, strive for heights, for nothing else compares,
To standing where ambition finds its crest.
The world adores the ones who break despair,
And crown their dreams with what they've earned the best.

Beneath the Surface

True beauty hides beneath the skin,
Beyond the crafted guise.
It dwells within the soul's deep core,
Where depth and truth arise.

The surface wears a transient mask,
A fleeting, hollow glow.
But underneath, the spirit shines
With light the eyes can't know.

It's found in hearts that beat with care,
In minds that dare to dream.
Not in the flawless lines we see,
But in what's yet unseen.

The perfect face may fade with time,
The fleeting bloom may fall.
Yet inner grace, with steadfast roots,

Will outlast years' cruel call.

True beauty whispers in the quiet,
Not shouting to the skies.
It's in the strength of silent acts,
And in the softest sighs.

To seek the depth beyond the skin,
Is to uncover gold.
For what we see is not the truth,
But only what's been told.

True beauty lies in humble hearts,
In lives both flawed and free.
It flourishes where love and trust
Like a carefully nurtured tree.

The Light Within

In obscure shadows, where fears dwell,
A flicker shines so true.
Through storms that rage and waves that toss,
Hope's light will guide us through.

When clouds obscure the brightest day,
And dreams seem far away,
A whisper rises in the heart,
To chase the dark away.

The road is long, the night is cold,
Yet dawn awaits the skies.
For every tear, a smile awaits,
To wipe the weary eyes.

Each step we take, though fraught with pain,
Unfolds a brighter scene.
The struggles now, though hard to bear,

Will shape what might have been.

For seeds of hope, though buried deep,
Will bloom when least we know.
And in the quiet of the night,
Our strength begins to grow.

Hold the torch and walk the path,
Though weary you may be.
The stars above will light your way,
To all you're meant to see.

In every heart, a fire burns bright,
No matter how it seems.
With optimism, life becomes
The canvas of your dreams.

Grateful Reflections

Beneath the veil of twilight's tender hue,
Where whispers soft in amber breezes flow,
Must reside a heart imbued with wonders true,
A wealth of treasures only few may know.

For precious moments kissed by nature's art,
The glimmering stardust strewn on velvet skies,
We hold an ever-reverent, steadfast heart,
The quiet echoes where my thanks are bred.

Though trials gnaw and shadows oft-beguile,
A grateful spirit stands, its beacon bright,
For in the tempest dwells a hidden smile,
And even darkness kneels to dawning light.

So here we stand, mere mortals in prayer,

To crown the simple gifts life bids, endure

For gratitude, a virtue beyond compare,

Transcends all wealth—eternal, strong, and pure.

Beneath the roof that shields from stormy skies,

A blessing rests where many find but none,

The warmth of hearth, the light in weary eyes,

A quiet joy for battles we have won.

Tender Mercies

Through shaded groves where tender mercies bloom,
Their whispers soothe the weary and the weak,
A solace found amidst the shadowed gloom,
A gentle strength for those too frail to speak.

The dawn may break with hues of muted gold,
Its warmth a promise wrought by unseen care,
A gift bestowed that cannot quite be told,
Yet lingers soft, like blessings in the air.

When storms assail and tears like rivers flow,
A calm descends to cradle every cry,
A mercy veiled, its path we may not know,
But feel its light when all seems dark and dry.

Each fragile grace, a thread of heaven's weave,
Unseen yet felt in every breath we take,

Evidence for those who still believe,

That love endures, though hearts may bend or break.

In the Light of Faith

When shadows fall and nights grow long,
And doubt creeps in, a silent thief,
Hold steadfast to your heart's bright song,
For hope will shield you from the grief.

When tempests rage and waters rise,
And all seems lost in life's cruel game,
Look not with fear into the skies,
But trust the stars will light your name.

Though weary steps may falter still,
And trials press with heavy weight,
The power rests within your will,
To claim your dreams, defy your fate.

So guard your faith through darkest days,
And let its light your path reveal,
For triumph blooms in steadfast ways,

When hearts believe and spirits heal.

In the Wake of Dreams

Dreams are the seeds of what could be,
A spark that lights the darkest night.
They paint a world we yearn to see,
A whispered hope, a guiding light.

But dreams alone won't forge the way,
They fade like mist at break of dawn.
It's action that will make them stay,
Transforming visions to the drawn.

Dare to dream, let passion soar,
But build with hands and steadfast will.
For dreams combined with effort's core
Can turn the void to something real.

Under the stars where dreams take flight,
A world unfolds in quiet streams.
A spark ignites within the night,

To bridge the gap from dreams to schemes.

The heart envisions boundless skies,
Where hope ascends on fragile wings.
Yet toil must weave what thought supplies,
To birth the truth ambition brings.

For dreams alone are fleeting mist,
A vision's glow, a whispered plea.
But action's hand and mind's assist,
Transform the dream to destiny.

Dream and let your spirit soar,
But build with care what you pursue.
For dreaming opens every door,
And effort lets you walk them through.

Toil's Harvest

Within the grasp of toil's unyielding hand

Lies dreams unshaped, awaiting fierce embrace.

Through trials vast, the steadfast make their stand,

Refusing ease, they carve their destined space.

No gilded path extends for those who strive,

But thorny trails where shadows loom and press.

Yet in such strain, the embers come alive,

Igniting fires that forge one's true success.

The fleeting mirth of idleness deceives,

A siren's song that fades with the passing tide.

Yet labour sows what fleeting joy achieves,

A harvest rich, where lasting fruits abide.

For grit transcends the bounds of fleeting fate,

Each drop of sweat is a bridge to distant dreams.

Endurance, crowned with patience, grows innate,

It's quiet strength flows deep in endless streams.

Through storms of doubt, the resolute prevail,

Their mettle tempered by the winds of strife.

Each failure bears the seed of next travail,

A stepping stone to elevate their life.

Thus, let no soul disdain the weight of care,

For burdens borne refine the roughest ore.

In hardship's crucible, the bold declare,

That toil alone unlocks ambition's door.

To those who labour, glory shall accrue,
For effort is the compass of the wise.
Through ceaseless work, horizons vast renew,
And hard-earned victory lights eternal skies.

Second Chances

A fleeting sun in shadowed skies,
A whisper through the storm,
Though time may falter, hope replies,
A chance that is to be reborn.

The roads we tread, so often steep,
With thorns that line the way,
Yet mercy finds us when we weep,
And turns the night into day.

Each fall, a lesson, though it stings,
Each tear, a cleansing rain,
For life, in second chances, brings
Magic to heal the pain.

So rise again with a steady heart,
Let burdens fall away,
For every ending plays its part

To shape a better day.

Beneath the weight of past mistakes,
A door swings open wide,
The world extends its gentle hand,
A guide through storms we hide.

The broken path we thought was lost,
Finds light along the bend,
For every fall, a chance to rise,
And start anew again.

The echoes of regret may fade,
As hope begins to bloom,
A second chance, a gift of grace,
Dispelling both doubt and gloom.

Embrace the blessing life bestows,
Its whispers soft and true,
Each second chance, a tender vow,
To manifest a life where hopes renew.

A Frenemy's Deceit

A fleeting laugh, a careless word,
It spreads like fire through hidden halls.
A voice unseen, yet always heard,
Its echo as sharp as canyon walls.

Behind closed doors, the shadows play,
With tongues that twist and subtly lie.
The truth is bent, its edges fray,
And friendships falter, left to die.

The ones who jest may never see,
The weight their venom truly bears.
For every cruel soliloquy,
Breeds broken trust and silent prayers.

With careless jest, the tongue may slide,
A cutting edge on fragile hearts.
The cruel delight that mocks with pride

Leaves scars where trust departs.

Beware the path where gossip thrives,
A tangled web where honour slips.
For what you mock in others' lives
May one day rest upon your lips.

So pause before the jest is cast,
And weigh the worth of fleeting cheer.
For kindness shown will ever last,
While slander fades, a shameful smear.

Goodness Always Boomerangs

Beneath the veil where fleeting shadows play,
The seeds of kindness find their hallowed ground.
Though veiled in time, they seek a brighter day,
To sprout anew where grace and good abound.

Each selfless act, though small and left unseen,
Creates a ripple through the boundless deep.
A whispered truth, a bond where hearts convene,
Its echoes linger, though the world may sleep.

The hands that offer aid, the hearts that heal,
Unfurl a tapestry of endless light.
For what is given with unfeigned appeal
Returns, unbidden, in the darkest night.

A quiet smile can bridge despair's abyss,
And turn the tide for souls adrift, alone.
The simplest gestures birth the grandest bliss,
A spark to kindle warmth in hearts of stone.

No earthly ledger keeps the tally true,
No scales can weigh the measure of the soul.
Yet good bestowed will, like the morning dew,
Return to quench the thirst and make us whole.

Through trials borne, the virtuous remain,
Their deeds are a beacon in the waning haze.
For even in the depths of loss and pain,
The seeds they planted flourish in their ways.

The winds may scatter what is freely sown,
Yet roots will take where fertile soil abides.
The fruits of kindness, though in silence grown,

Will find their way, no matter where one hides.

Thus, let our hands be gentle, hearts sincere,
And offer light where shadows twist and moan.
For every act of good, distant or near,
Will find its path and make its sender known.

The universe, a mirror to our deeds,
Reflects the love and grace that we bestow.
From humble roots to everlasting seeds,
The good we give will always have its rewards in tow.

The Turning Tide of Time

The tide of time, so sly and fleet,
Now shifts to lift the quiet voice,
The overlooked find steady feet,
As fate unfolds its cunning choice.

The meek who stood with a trembling hand,
Find strength where whispers gently grew,
The shifting grains of time's vast sand,
Now carve a path for something new.

Those ignored by watchful eyes,
Now claim the heights they dared not dream,
While mighty walls and subtle sighs
Are swept away by time's swift stream.

Beware of the words we cast in spite,
For time's great tide is prone to turn,

What once was shadow takes to flight,
And dimming stars now brightly burn.

A seed dismissed as weak and small
Can root and break the strongest stone,
The ones we mock may one day call
A throne of triumph all their own.

The whispered scorn, the fleeting jest,
Might echo louder than we know,
For those we judge as second-best
May rise and let their power show.

So wield your tongue with gentle art,
Lest time should pierce your humbled heart.
Let the doubted now embrace
Their rightful, long-deserving place.

What Grace Looks Like

Through trials vast, she stands serene,
A protective shelter in the storm's embrace,
Her grace a balm for every pain,
Her courage carved from time and space.

Her hands, though worn, still softly weave,
A tapestry of love so wide,
Through every tear, she dares to believe,
And keeps her faith as storms collide.

Her voice, a calm and soothing stream,
Dispels the weight of fear and loss,
Her gaze reflects a quiet dream,
Advising that life is but a game of pitch and toss.

In giving, she transcends her plight,
A heart unyielding, vast and whole,

Transforming darkness into light,
Her spirit, anchor to the soul.

She finds in sorrow seeds to sow,
A garden blooming through despair,
Her strength a river's steady flow,
A testament to love's repair.

Oh, mother, graceful, generous guide,
Your trials bear a sacred art,
In you, both grace and strength reside,
A boundless gift, a beating heart.

Inimitable Indulgence

A guiding hand both firm and kind,
You lead with wisdom, calm and true.
A voice of reason, open mind,
In every choice, we turn to you.

You listen well, with patience rare,
Each thought, each word, you weigh with care.
No dream too small, no view unfair,
A gem like you found nowhere.

In your embrace, we've grown so free,
Encouraged by your steady heart.
Your greatest gift, democracy,
That binds us close yet sets apart.

You listen well to every voice,
Each thought you honour, every plea.
In you, we find the power of choice,

A gift of trust, a path to be.

In every deed, your truth shines bright,
Your word, a bond that will not break.
With integrity, you do what is right,
With honesty, no choice to fake.

Your mind, so sharp and wise,
With knowledge vast and clear as day.
You see the world with thoughtful eyes,
Your intelligence guides our way.

Forever grateful, we remain,
For all you are, for all you've done.
A father's love, a sweet refrain,
A guiding star for everyone.

Appreciation for The Gift of Love

I never knew a feeling so deep,
Like a treasure that my heart would keep,
In every glance, in every sigh,
I find my soul reaching for the sky.

To love, it feels like floating free,
Like waves that kiss the endless sea,
A warmth that wraps me, soft and true,
In every thought, I think of you.

You fill the spaces, quiet, wide,
With tender words I can't deny,
And in your eyes, I see the sun,
A world that's bright, where we are one.

It's in the laughter, it's in the touch,
The way you care, I feel so much.

When storms begin to cloud the mind—
In love, a peace I've come to find.

So here I stand, no need to roam,
For love with you feels like home,
I'll cherish it, this gift so pure,
In this love, it feels secure.

True love is not a fading flame,
Not bound by time, it stakes its claim.
In your loving presence, I never tire,
For your love is life's force multiplier.

Printed by Libri Plureos GmbH in Hamburg,
Germany